Veggie Friends
and Fruits too!

A Children's Cookbook
on Creating Healthy Snacks

BY ANNE LEGGE

I dedicate this cookbook to
my beautiful children, Jack and Eliza.
You will always be my greatest inspiration.
And to my husband, David, for always supporting me in
my artistic endeavors.

Introduction

Ever been told by your mother not to play with your food? Well, forget it! This cookbook shows you how to make fun creatures with your vegetables and fruits to play with and gobble up. These colorful pages teach you to be creative with food and stay on the path of good nutrition. You will need an adult to help you cut your vegetables and fruits but making the snack will be up to you. So bring your imagination and appetite for some good fun with food.

This cookbook is great for parties or just fun snack time. Enjoy watching your child create veggie and fruit friends that make eating nutritionally a cinch.

Tools

To get started making your tasty snacks you will need a few tools. Make sure to ask an adult to help you since these tools can be sharp and dangerous if not handled properly.

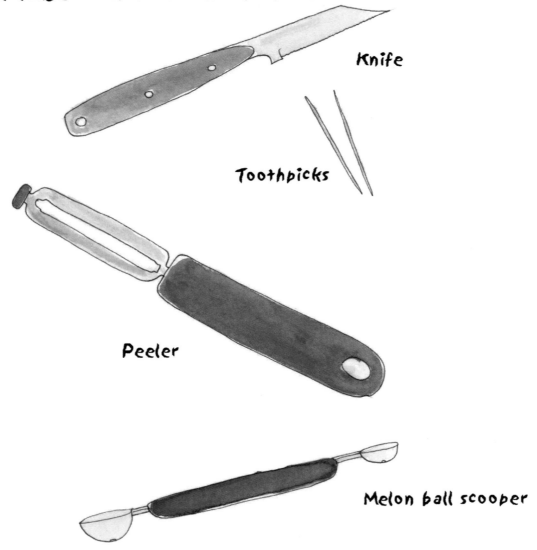

Knife

Toothpicks

Peeler

Melon ball scooper

Bighorn Sheep

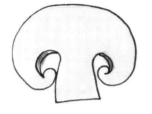

1 Mushroom
2 Florets of Cauliflower

Wash all vegetables before starting. Stand the mushroom up on the stem and cut it lengthwise until you have a nice large slice with the stem and cap intact. Next, take 2 large florets of cauliflower and lay them stem side down on the surface. These are the body of the sheep. Then place the mushroom slice in front of the body as the head. Look at those large horns!

Bird

1 Watermelon
1 Peach
1 Strawberry

Wash all fruits before starting. First, cut the peach in half and discard the pit. Then cut slices out of the halves. Peel the skin off two slices. Lay them down so they make a circle. This is the body of the bird. Next, cut the top off the strawberry and lay it on its side. Slice through the strawberry, widthwise, to get wheel shapes. Take the largest one and lay it in front of the body as the head. Then slice a piece of watermelon. Slice it again so you have a triangle for the tail. Cut the rind off and place it behind the body. Take another slice and cut out three small triangles for the beak and feet. Make a flock of birds!

Butterfly #1

1 Yellow bell pepper
1 Green bean
1-2 Pimento stuffed olives
1 Carrot

First, wash all your vegetables. Next, cut off the ends of the green bean and lay it down as the body of the butterfly. Then cut the top off the bell pepper, scrape out the seeds, and lay it on its side. Next, cut a slice of the bell pepper. Take that slice and cut it in half. Lay each half down on either side of the green bean as wings. Next, take the olive and thinly slice through, trying to keep the red pimento in the middle of each slice. You may need to slice two olives to get four good slices. Place the slices in the tips of the wings. Finally, take your carrot, peel away the outer skin. Then make a few more peels to use as antennas. Place them above the body. Next, cut the remainder of the carrot into small, thin slivers and arrange them inside the wings to create a nice pattern. Good job!

Butterfly #2

1 Orange
2 Blueberries
1 Banana

First, wash all of your fruit. Then peel and section the orange. Next, take two sections and cut them in half widthwise. Then peel the banana and cut it in half. Then cut that half lengthwise. Lay the flat side down on your work surface as the body of your butterfly. Then lay the orange sections next to the banana as wings. Finally, place the blueberries at the top as eyes. Enjoy!

Cat

1 Nectarine
1 Slice of cantaloupe
2 Dried cranberries

Wash all of the fruit before starting.
Cut the nectarine in half and
discard the pit. Lay one half,
flat side down, as your body. Next,
cut a slice out of the other half for
the tail. Cut it again so that it can
fit alongside your body. Then cut
another slice of nectarine and slice
the two ends off for ears. Place
them above the head. Next, scoop
out and discard the seeds of the
cantaloupe. Then, using your melon
scooper, make one large ball for
the head. Next, make two small
balls for the legs. Finally, add two
cranberries as the feet. Meow!

Caterpillar

1 Plum tomato
1 Radish
6-8 Soy beans/ edamame
2 Sunflower sprouts

Wash all of your vegetables.
First, take the plum tomato
and put it on its side. Cut
off the top and bottom.
Then cut the remaining
piece in half widthwise.
Take each half, lay them
flat and cut them in half
again. Next, scoop out the
seeds and discard. Lay the
four pieces down and line
them up in a row. Then
place the soybeans
inbetween each section of
the tomato to create feet.
Then cut the top and bottom
off the radish and place it
in front of the tomato.
Finally, take a toothpick
and pierce the radish on
top. Carefully place sprout
antennas in the holes. Now
you can inch your way
toward healthy eating.

Chick

1 Apricot
1 Banana

Wash all the fruit before starting.
Cut the apricot in half and discard
the pit. Lay one half, flat side down,
on your work surface. Next, peel the
banana. Cut a wheel slice and lay it
flat. Then cut a triangle out of the
wheel as the beak. Cut two more
wheels and make two more triangles
for feet. Place the feet below the
body and the beak on the side.
There is your chick!

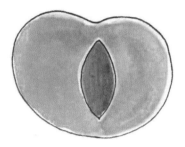

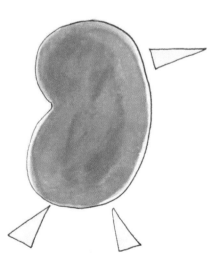

Chicken

1 Pear
1 Strawberry
1 Banana

Start with washing all of your fruit. Use a knife to slice the pear lengthwise. Use a melon scooper or the tip of a peeler to take out the center seeds of the pear. Then lay your pear flat side down with the small end facing up. This is the body of your chicken. Next, peel the banana and slice off a few wheels. Then, cut out some feet and a beak for your chicken. Finally cut off the top of a strawberry and cut it lengthwise into 3-4 slices. Place one at the top of the body with the small end up. Then take another slice and place it on the side of the pear just under the beak. Enjoy!

Crab

1 Plum tomato
1 Red bell pepper

Wash all vegetables before starting. Cut the top off of the tomato. Then place it flat side down, as the body of the crab. Next, cut off the top of the pepper. Remove and discard seeds. Then lay the pepper on its side and cut slices. Next, cut those slices in half. These are the legs. Arrange the pepper slices so that they are standing up and coming away from the body. Now you have a crab!

Dragonfly

1 Orange
2 Blueberries
8-10 Raspberries

First, wash all of your fruit. Next, peel the orange and separate it into sections. Then take off any stems still attached to the raspberries and line them up as the body. Then lay the orange sections down as the wings. Finally, place the two blueberries next to the head of your body as the eyes. Super job!

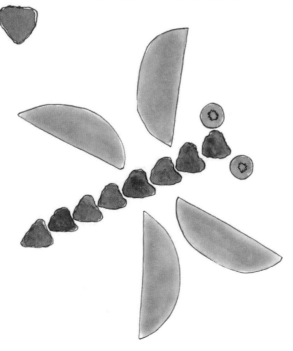

Duck

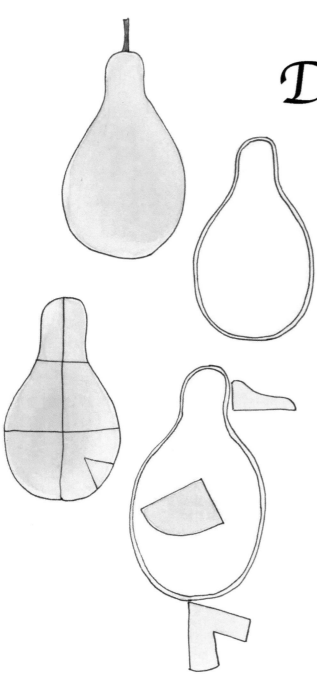

1 Yellow pear

Wash all fruit before starting. First, stand the pear upright and slice downward right next to the stem. Then take the half without the stem, stand it upright, and slice it again making a thin slice. That slice can be laid down as the body of the duck. Then take the remainder of the slice and lay it flat. Cut it once lengthwise and twice widthwise. (See drawing on left) Then cut a small triangle out of the big section. Then take one of the small sections and lay it down as the beak. Then take one of the big sections and use it as the wing. Finally, take the section with the cutout triangle and place it at the bottom of the body as the feet. Enjoy!

Fish

1 Melon
1 Peach or nectarine

The fish is easy! First wash your fruit. Then cut a wedge out of the melon and discard the seeds. Next, use your melon scooper to make balls out of the melon for the bodies of the fish. Then cut the nectarine in half and discard the pit. Then slice sections out of the halves and use them as tails. Assemble and enjoy your school of fish!

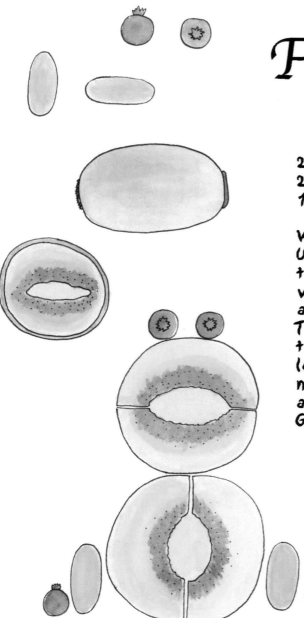

Frog

2 Blueberries
2 Green seedless grapes
1 Kiwi fruit

Wash all of your fruit before starting.
Using your knife, peel the skin off
the kiwi fruit. Then cut the fruit into
wheels. Lay two wheels down, one
as the head and one as the body.
Then take the two grapes and place
them on either side of the body as
legs. Lastly, place two blueberries
next to the legs as feet, and two
as eyes on top of the head.
Good Work!

Ladybug

1 Grape tomato
1 Jumbo black olive
2 Sunflower sprouts

Start with washing all of your vegetables. First, cut slits on either side of the jumbo black olive and slowly push the tomato into the olive. As the tomato is pushed forward the olive should give way and expand around the tomato. This should look like wings. Finally, take a toothpick and make two small holes on the top of the olive. Place the two sunflower sprouts in the holes as antennas. Good enough to eat!

Lizard

1 Zucchini
5 Green beans
1 Pea
1 Red bell pepper

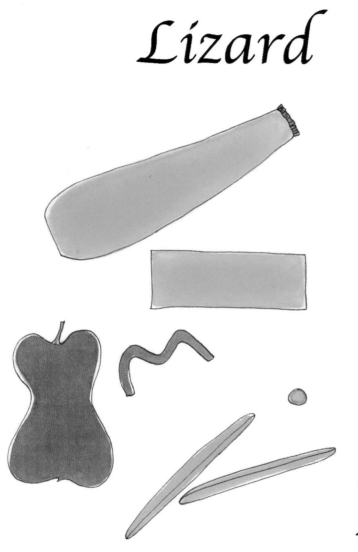

Wash all vegetables before starting. Cut the top and bottom off the zucchini. Then cut it in half widthwise. Next, take one half and cut it lengthwise. Lay that half flat on your work surface as your body. Then take four green beans and cut them in half. Take the last green bean and cut it into fourths. Stack two of the beans in front of the body as the head. Then stack three of the beans at the back of the body as the start of the tail. Then add two more and then one. Your tail is now complete. Then take the last four pieces of beans and place them down as feet. Next, take your pepper and cut it widthwise. Cut a thin slice from one of the halves. Then cut that slice in half again. Lay that slice in front of the head as the tongue. Finally, add the pea as the eye.

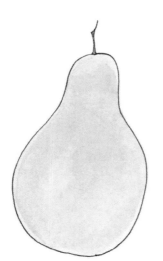

Mouse

1 Pear
9 Dried cranberries
1 Raisin

Wash the pear before starting.
Cut the pear lengthwise, then
cut that half lengthwise again.
Next, peel the skin off that quarter
with a peeler or a knife. Lay the
pear slice down flat on a surface.
That is the body of the mouse. Next,
take the dried cranberries and make
a tail for the mouse by arranging
them behind the body. Finally, place
the raisin in front as the nose. Squeak!

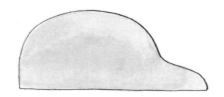

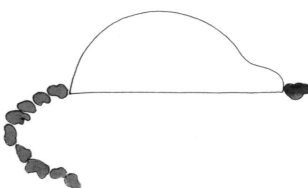

Octopus

1 Floret of broccoli
8 Green beans

Wash all the vegetables before
starting. Take the broccoli floret
and cut the stem straight across
so it can stand up on a flat surface.
Cut and discard the tips of the
green beans. Now, set up the
broccoli on your work surface and
lay the eight beans around as
tentacles. Yummy!

Owl

1 Apple
4 Raisins
1 Banana
1 Slice of pineapple

Wash all fruits before starting.
Slice the apple lengthwise. Then
slice it again so you have a thin
slice to work with. Cut that slice
in half lengthwise and discard
the seeds and core. Place the two
halves back together to create the
face. Take the whole slice of pineapple
and place it below the apple slices
as the body. Then peel the banana
and cut it in half. Then slice the
half lengthwise. Lay the slices, flat
side down, on top of the pineapple
as wings. Finally, take the four raisins
and place two on the apples as eyes
and two below the body as feet.
Tasty!

Rabbit

2 Florets of cauliflower
1 Radish

Wash all vegetables before
starting. Take a large floret
of cauliflower and lay it down
on your work surface as the body.
Then cut a small floret of cauliflower
and lay it behind the body as
the tail. Next, cut the top off
the radish. Lay the radish on its
side and cut three thin slices. Lay
one slice down as the head. Take
another slice and cut an arch to
create an ear. Place that above
the head, and repeat with the
last radish slice. Now you can
hop your way to good nutrition.

Sheep

2 Florets of cauliflower
1 Jumbo black olive

Wash all of your vegetables. Cut the end off the jumbo olive so you have a flat surface on one end. Then arrange the two florets of cauliflower down and place the flat side of the olive against one cauliflower as the head. Healthy fun!

Snail

1 Radish
1 Green bean
2 Sunflower sprouts

Wash all vegetables before beginning. First, take the radish and cut off the top. Then carve a line across the top of the radish, using the tip of your peeler or a knife. You want the line to be wide and deep enough to fit around the green bean. Then assemble the snail by placing the green bean on your work surface and fitting the radish on top, aligning the carved out area with the body of the green bean. Then use a toothpick to make two holes on either side of the green bean and insert sprouts as the antennas. That was fun!

Snake

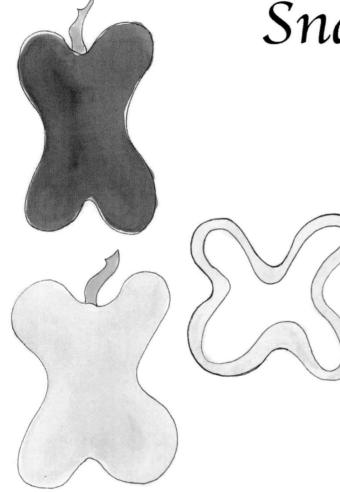

1 Red bell pepper
1 Yellow bell pepper

Wash your vegetables before starting. Use a knife and cut off the tops of both peppers. Then scoop out the seeds and discard them. Place the peppers on their sides and cut them into thin slices. Then quarter the slices so you have four arches per slice. Finally, arrange the arches next to each other to make a slithering snake.

Spider

1 Cucumber

First, wash the cucumber. Then peel the skin and cut off the two ends. Next, cut one thick slice off the end and set it aside. Then cut the cucumber lengthwise. Using a spoon, scoop out the seeds and discard. Then cut 1/2 inch thick slices. These will be the legs. Take the whole slice you cut earlier and cut it in half. Set it upright on your work surface, flat side down, as the body. Then arrange the legs around the body. Now you have a scary snack!

Starfish

1 Orange
1 Cherry

Wash all fruit before you begin.
Peel and section the orange.
Then arrange five sections in
a circle leaving room in the
center for the body. Next, cut
the cherry in half and take the
pit out. Use one half and lay it
flat in the center of the orange
sections. Now you have a
starfish.

Swan

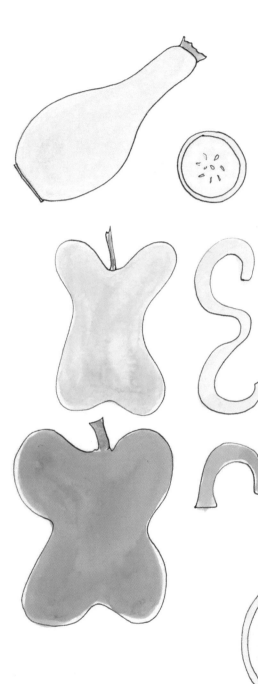

1 Yellow squash
1 Yellow bell pepper
1 Green bell pepper

First wash all of your vegetables. Then slice the squash into wheels. Next, place a large wheel down as the body of your duck. Then cut the tops off the peppers and discard the seeds. Next, lay the peppers on their sides and cut thin slices. Finally, cut those slices into quarters and arrange one as the wing and one as the head. Great job!

Turtle #1

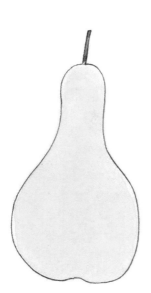

1 Pear
1 Strawberry

Start by washing your fruit. Then slice the pear in half lengthwise. Next, use a peeler tip or a melon scooper to take out the seeds of the pear. Then lay the pear flat and cut it lengthwise again. Now you have the body of the turtle. Next, take the top off the strawberry and slice it lengthwise. Take the two slices and lay them at the bottom of the body as feet. Delicious!

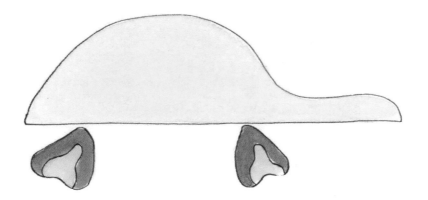

Turtle #2

1 Avocado
1 Radish

Wash all your fruits and vegetables before starting. Cut the avocado in half lengthwise. Then cut it in half again. Remove the pit and discard. Lay that quarter down on a flat surface as the body of the turtle. Then slice the radish widthwise into thin slices. Next, take a slice and cut off each side of the radish at an angle, so you have a smaller top than bottom. Lay that slice under the body as one foot. Repeat that cut with another slice of radish for the other foot. You are so creative!

Whale

1 Plum
6 Seedless red grapes
30 Blueberries (depending on size)

Wash all fruit before starting.
Cut the plum in half, lengthwise,
and remove the pit. Lay one half
down flat and cut the tail out, as
indicated in the drawing. Next,
arrange the grapes as the inside
of the body. Then take the
blueberries and push them around
the grapes to form the biggest
whale you want. Lastly, attach the
tail to the end of your whale and
enjoy!

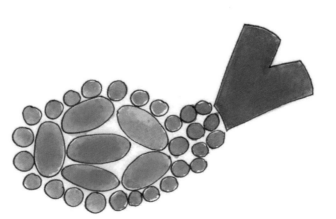